SIDE EFFECTS MAY INCLUDE STRANGERS

T0096464

THE HUGH MACLENNAN POETRY SERIES

Editors: Allan Hepburn and Carolyn Smart

Titles in the series
Waterglass Jeffery Donaldson
All the God-Sized Fruit Shawna Lemay
Chess Pieces David Solway
Giving My Body to Science Rachel Rose
The Asparagus Feast S.P. Zitner
The Thin Smoke of the Heart Tim Bowling
What Really Matters Thomas O'Grady
A Dream of Sulphur Aurian Haller
Credo Carmine Starnino
Her Festival Clothes Mavis Jones
The Afterlife of Trees Brian Bartlett
Before We Had Words S.P. Zitner
Bamboo Church Ricardo Sternberg
Franklin's Passage David Solway
The Ishtar Gate Diana Brebner
Hurt Thyself Andrew Steinmetz
The Silver Palace Restaurant Mark Abley
Wet Apples, White Blood Naomi Guttman
Palilalia Jeffery Donaldson
Mosaic Orpheus Peter Dale Scott
Cast from Bells Suzanne Hancock
Blindfold John Mikhail Asfour
Particles Michael Penny
A Lovely Gutting Robin Durnford
The Little Yellow House Heather Simeney MacLeod
Wavelengths of Your Song Eleonore Schönmaier
But for Now Gordon Johnston
Some Dance Ricardo Sternberg

Side Effects
May Include Strangers

DOMINIK PARISIEN

McGill-Queen's University Press
Montreal & Kingston • London • Chicago

ISBN 978-0-2280-0357-1 (paper)
ISBN 978-0-2280-0499-8 (ePDF)
ISBN 978-0-2280-0500-1 (ePUB)

Legal deposit fourth quarter 2020
Bibliothèque nationale du Québec

Printed in Canada on acid-free paper that is 100% ancient forest free
(100% post-consumer recycled), processed chlorine free

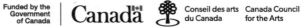

Financé par le   Funded by the   Conseil des arts   Canada Council
gouvernement   Government   du Canada   for the Arts
du Canada   of Canada

We acknowledge the support of the Canada Council for the Arts.

Nous remercions le Conseil des arts du Canada de son soutien.

Library and Archives Canada Cataloguing in Publication

Title: Side effects may include strangers/Dominik Parisien.

Names: Parisien, Dominik, author.

Series: Hugh MacLennan poetry series.

Description: Series statement: The Hugh MacLennan poetry series |
Poems.

Identifiers: Canadiana (print) 20200312197 | Canadiana (ebook)
20200312359 | ISBN 9780228003571 (paper) |
ISBN 9780228004998 (PDF) | ISBN 9780228005001 (ePUB)

Classification: LCC PS8631.A7469 S53 2020 | DDC C811/.6—dc23

This book was typeset by Marquis Interscript in 9.5/13 Sabon.

what is a poem is inside of your body
bpNichol

So sorry you understand this
Roxanna Bennett

I love the art of us. To one another, we are galleries
of solidarity.
Imani Barbarin

CONTENTS

PAIN BY ANY OTHER NAME

LET US FOR A MOMENT CALL THIS PAIN
BY OTHER WORDS

Ask, *How many roses does the hammer weigh*
when it bears down on your skull?

Does the sword seem toothed like a toddler's smile
or sharp as your first ice skates?

On a scale of anglerfish to northern lights
how bright are the flashes in your head?

When I touch this, here, which constellations
light the sky behind your eyes?

Would you say that pulsing is the flicker of a satellite
or the stubborn heartbeat of a newborn chick?

Ask, *Can we for a moment make of beauty*
the measure of our pain? and I will answer.

Maybe pain is a prayer
the body makes. Ungrateful
god, would you deny hallelujahs
of red, red worship?

BILINGUAL PATHWAYS

"French people are so hardcore they eat
        pain for breakfast"

pain by any other name would still be
                                    bread
can we unlanguage
                associative pathway
unfeel
into sourdough
     rye
            pumpernickel
rewrite
   golden crust
 carbohydrate
         as synaptic
truth

Pain is just a delusion
the mind indulges. Impression-
able fool, why pantomime living
a wronged, wronged body?

(B)RAIN WEATHER

now right now

the words for migraine
are metaphor

a rat drowning in jelly

a failed ice pick lobotomy

brain weather

this poem carving itself
into your skull

words are artificial
constructs we impose
on natural phenomena
        so a simile
like lightning-struck sand
crystallizing   in the process
of becoming fulgurite
        would work too

so long as something
violently becomes something
else
        all of you
        as only brain weather

it really is
difficult to word
when you become the rain

Child, your body is not only metaphor.
Tell us, do you conjure pain in older forms?
As hammer, fire, anvil, nail? As knife?

Imagine a picture book of pain:

could we call this ache a cactus, a chinchilla,
a diamond, or that ill a mole rat, a rainbow,
a nebula? Does it hop, skip, dig, or shine?

This too is life, child. Learn the words and then
invent your own.

IT IS NOT THIS?

A poem the universe
composes. We are all subjects
of pain, its pen & paper, & are
each read & worth reading.

understand
none of this
is a call to silence

understand
we too can sing
of balmy bruise & burn & ache

understand
pain is a privilege
when chosen

WITH APOLOGIES TO THOSE
WITH CONGENITAL ANALGESIA

Note: the rules of the dance are simple: if the caller announces a
circumstance that has occurred in the lifetime of you or your
partner, you must leave the dance floor at once.

Anyone with pain

Michael Ondaatje, *Elimination Dance*

Eliminating those with pain
leaves no one behind.

The dance proclaims we are one
in this experience,
esoteric & mundane as it is.

This companionship says nothing
of degree.

Compare a sore tooth to a seizure.
Broken clavicle to cystic fibrosis.
Stubbed toe to fibromyalgia.

Say you never danced to begin with,
in pain enough you couldn't.

Watched with equal guilt & envy,
congenital analgesia on your mind,
that with it you might have danced
& danced & danced

& never even known
you ached.

UN DOCTEUR ANGLOPHONE
TRADUIT LES INQUIÉTUDES DE SON PATIENT
AVEC GOOGLE

écoute
à quoi bon être poète

beau dire
ce mal
semble dans la tête comme
marteau feu enclume clou couteau
ou l'éclat d'une baudroie ou des
aurores boréales

à la fin
pour ce qui importe
on fait toujours mauvaise traduction
la douleur est une langue
où les mots sont minable tentative
à ce qu'on ne peut que vivre
dans le corps

écoute
docteur
toi qui connais
la souffrance
dis
simplement
ce mal d'aujourd'hui
je
m'en
tirerais
avec de l'aide
ou
est-ce une
peine de
mort

AN ENGLISH-SPEAKING DOCTOR
TRANSLATES THE CONCERNS OF HIS PATIENT
WITH GOOGLE

listening
what good is being poet

beautiful say
this pain
seems in the head like
hammer fire anvil nail knife
or the brilliance of a monkfish or
northern Lights

at the end
for what matters
we always do bad translation
pain is a language
where the words are shabby attempt
we can only live
in the body

listening
doctor
you who know
suffering
tell
simply
this evil of today
I
me
would shoot
with help
or
is it a
trouble
death

Maybe pain is
~~a poem~~
~~a prayer~~
~~a delusion~~

Maybe pain is

_____

_____

_____

Maybe pain is.

STRANGE(R) BODIES

THE BODY CALLS FOR GUESTS

Illness a synonym
      for open.
Invitation
to pills, procedures, home-
made salves & solutions.
The world hears
Welcome,
      Welcome,
and enters.

A body is lightning in a bottle.
Some small miracle,
a sequence of events
necessary for one.
All of them political.
Especially those that aren't.
The word strains like us
to contain multitudes, defining
one thing against another.
Me. A mass. A thing passed
or a thing of importance. Both
boundary
& boundless.

They always fear
        the liminal
& you   they say
are a tributary
   too fluid
to be anything
but potential
for a flood.

What they really mean is
        they don't know
how to swim
in another.

a k leans like a held knife
straight line with steel blade
& handle halfway open

everything a metaphor
even letters catch the light
of an unsheathed knife

q a queer boy's guts spilling
out a belly &
there & there & there the knife

was there always violence
hidden in the words
unthink back to ignorance

this nightmare alphabet all
angled wrong slashing
everywhere & queer boy guts

spilling spilling spilling out
of everything &
there a knife a knife a knife

THE WALL SPELLED LOVE

I learned jealousy
reading of a boy who kissed
a wall.

Oliver kissed here
scribbled on the brick.
I knew, then, love was breathing

yourself into another;
how boys feared getting caught
losing themselves through their lips.

And here was Oliver,
who could have carried me
with him forever,

giving himself away
to a red brick wall.

PENNY

There is no magic in the world
but this: her, sowing copper-plated dreams on concrete &
    gravel.

She divines by a flick of her wrist, by the ring of coin on
    ground
when none watch, thinking, *Investments in folklore*
profit everyone.

At night she dreams of rusted coins melting
into grasping hands, of bloodstreams thick
with wishes.

ABLEIST ANALYSIS

Imagine! A time when a body
might have been made myth,
conduit to a god, symbol
of the wrath, will, blessing of a greater force
for its difference. Signifier:
coward father; faithless mother;
culture's sin made manifest.
Stand-in for entire worlds, able
to imbue meaning to all things
but itself.

The myth of body
      is this
impermeable
place
this state
      of being
never porous
when the *me*
      is almost
wholly
made up
      of others.

WHAT YOU LEARN, DROWNING

Lungs full of river
his lips breathe
into me new life.

AFTER DECIDING NOT TO DIE BY SUICIDE, YOU SHOULD BE THINKING

of all the usual gratitudes. Too often
is it really life you live is asked of you & yours;
tragedy their anticipated narrative.

> Cue slow pan on some bottles.
> Hint of bluish arm.
> Dramatic fade to black.

Consider: can you be disabled & contribute
something new on suicide, or will all your words
read tragic, even when they celebrate?

Are you writing using *you* through empathy or cowardice?
If in weariness you call the poem just a poem
even once, what harm will that denial cause?

Facing suicide, are unanswerable questions
the only ones worth asking?

Worth ending with?

SIDE EFFECTS MAY INCLUDE STRANGERS

informing you the pills are like a god
you might not worship now but will
in time; how the way of weakness
lies in relying on such artificial things;
how breathing on the sacred mountainside
of some great distant land cured their friend's
friend's uncle of some strange ailment;
or, that illness becomes a crucible only
if allowed.

o
let us be like you
flawed
failures
singular
    & successful
none of us
a credit
or exception
stand-in
or paragon
enough
to be
unremarkable
    & common
as a cold
enough
to make monoliths

meaningless

o
let us be like you
atoms
orbiting each other
subjects to the laws
of gravity
      & attraction

chemical
        & true
to our nature

o
let us be
let us be
let us be

I like to fuck in protest of this body.

I'm told the caring treatment afforded
my unconscious self
is a testament
to the kindness of strangers. I do see in it hope
& my own dissolution. Convulsing, I lose
the possessive body, become
a receptacle for concern, just a thing
touched everywhere through kindness
left perfumed with the sweat of another's care.

I seem ungrateful because I am
permeable in those moments,
a body bursting with strangers.

Sex is then the privilege of choosing
who participates in the choreography
of my limbs. My partner's hands
become a knife, carving other fingers from my skin
to help me shape myself again.

METAMORPHOSIS

TO A CHRONICALLY PAINED BODY

You modern Ovid, you are the tales

& the teller. Pain made metaphor is

pain made real. Reality seldom allows

for it without language. & once worded,

metamorphosis follows. Many will

make of you a narrative. Some curiosity

to interpret. Split the parts apart

for meaning. Question the analysis.

Then comes another with new

interpretation. Definitive theories. Always

back to meaning. And you, called mal-

functioning machine, broken engine, or

some other thing in this new vernacular.

Remember: you have a name. You are

that body, yes, & that story & more & more

& more.

MY PARTNER MAKES OF ME A POEM

a found poem, with Kelsi Morris

there's a lot of forest in you
you have the universe
        in one eye
the underside
    of a mushroom
in the other
there's a tree
hidden in your face
        that will outlive
        the world's end
the tree is asymmetrical & upright   bare
    though
  sometimes burst blood vessels
bloom like leaves
        on your forehead
I mean all of you is beautiful
but this rib here should really be a jewel
        around my neck
I'm partly made of you anyway
if I touch here
that scar is like a ravine
    I can't help but explore
from there I see the perfect clouds
    of your ears
& your freckles like stars

CAN WE CALL THIS AN AUBADE

here comes the dawn let's sleepless watch it rise you know i
want to write about the pills the way you greet the morning
with chemicals the way i do as an aubade & yes one of us
would need to leave for an aubade but i think i'm thinking
past that point well into the rituals of morning so maybe not
an aubade but i love the word because of l'aube & dawn can
be a name mais l'aube peut seulement être le matin ou un
poème if you bade it & i appreciate the succinctness of pills
you know you pronounce pillules with a lull pillull & yes
i'm rambling across languages again i know we could maybe
fuck away the dawn but desire lulls like the moon or pills &
nothing is profound or painless at dawn & i don't mean pills
lull desire our bodies are too tangled in insomnia anyway
& besides you hold a pill like the moon on your tongue there
one moment gone the next & then comes the day bright
& beautiful like you & yes my pills are in the other room
someday i want an art exhibit where portraits of pills by
bedsides flank smiling faces & the caption asks who are they
for & they're for all the faces & all the faces are couples &
can we call this an aubade if i leave to get my pills & come
back with birdsong & painkillers on my tongue i can put my
pills beside your own for the exhibit & l'aube is well past &
you've left me here with pills for your dreams so i'll call this
an aubade & kiss you good morning & goodbye

It knows poetry
is subjective, how one creature's poem
is the art that beats at the heart of another.

At times it fancies itself a fanged Eliot,
ripping subject from context
to gestate new meaning.

It remembers hungering
for a greater capacity for abstraction,
how as it ate it dreamt
of expanding to encompass thoughts
on all things that never were.

(It mastered only the delicate methods
of outrageous violence.)

It believes an aesthetic
appreciation of the monstrous
is not for their like; that the day they explore
the canvas of its body
will reveal nothing
they would call wondrous.

A MASK IS NOT A FACE

My skinless daughter is sewing
a mask from broad-winged butterflies.

She lures them with lemon peel
milkweed goldenrod & sand
rolled in a ball balanced on her tongue
snaps her mouth shut like a flytrap
when their wings touch her palate
chuckles as their tongues suck
at air between her teeth
before she does what she does
with them.

Pierced by copper-headed pins
they cover the table
like newspapers for a papier-mâché collage
(she sometimes dips her fingers
in flour & water
and lets the mixture dry
like skin that cracks when she moves).

I have heard it said
(poor girl)
that she looks
like half a blood orange
like Mars through a telescope
like the underside of autumn leaves
& roadside carrion.

But when I ask & even when I don't
she lies and says
Don't worry and *I'm fine*
and keeps sewing that butterfly mask
(such a pretty thing such a smiling thing)
with its too-bright eyes & its too-wide lips.

I would tell her
a mask is not a face
it is a lie
but
when the wings are all sewn
and a lace knot tied behind the ears
she hands me the mask says
Here
so you'll smile more.

NIECE WITH A PEACH FOLLOWING FOUR MINUTES OF PLANET EARTH

nails & plastic cutlery
cut & stab & tear
the skin

at three she has teeth
like a beast & the instinct
to mutilate

understands implicitly she
is a predator at the dinner table
& survival is sinking

herself tooth & nail &
plastic tools deep
into fuzzy little things

I wish you disease
disability
for a day

I wish you impotence
the powerlessness
of pain

I wish never wanting to wish
illness on another
were true

I wish you sympathy
shifting into
empathy

I wish you understanding

I AM LEARNING TO FORGET

I hear the best werewolves are bilingual
        that there are wordstones inlaid in their cheeks
        with which their teeth stay sharp
        that their forked tongues can translate
        days into nights, nights into days.

In my mouth is an enduring summer solstice
where dawn follows dusk in such rapid succession
I barely taste the night.

When I howl my voice no longer carries.
My teeth do not break skin.

i would call you but my head is a balloon & the cellphone
light is a needle. a needling light. i need light but i don't think
you want me to pop. then again i don't know what I think.
a pop might do me good. i would write you but my balloon
is only tethered by a spinal string & now it's caught up in a
corner with the cobwebs & the dust. the oxygen is thin here
& i might be high from being high. still, i wish I could tell
you a story. i can't, while my head is a balloon. balloons
aren't very good with words – we're nothing but hot air. if
the air left my mouth, i might come down, but i don't think
I have a mouth. you should know – my elastic skull is
wearing at the ceiling. it is bumpy, sort of misshapen – the
ceiling – i mean, my head too, probably. got shoulders white
with dandelion stuff – no – with ceiling fluff like dandruff.
dandelions are for a world beyond the windows. at least
i can fly. or maybe float. flies fly. flies don't wear through
ceilings like balloons though. we'd see the sun through
our roofs if they could. needling sunlight piercing through,
popping us balloons. you know, it doesn't feel healthy, a
balloon trapped inside this way. do we balloons even have
eyes to be needled, or do we just think we do? maybe that's
really how balloons end, not with a sunlit pop, but with a
whisper. just that low sound of a balloon wearing through
a ceiling, until it reaches sky, floats/flies away & someone,
maybe you, looks up & whispers: hey, I could see my house
from there. not that i could hear you – we balloons have no
ears. all balloons have are thoughts, i think. & that's all we
can do. think.

tar
tarped
trapped
in
rain fig
brain fig
brain frog
brain fog
i hop
you under sand
sink stuck
what
i me main
by brain flog is
i fell
disco
neck net ted
no no
feel
earthed
unearthed
unteethed
untethered
untethered
a frag
fragile
thing rhino
rye now
end

i wan to be
tethered
aging again
my whirls
are words are
errant
right
right now
young know
like learning
a
land
gauge
language
where a
world
seems so sin
pull
just
one thing
until you
wrong it write
it sway it say
it wrong
car
crack it
open
end
all me
more
meaning
spills

out

ARACHNOID CYST

The boy knows arachnoid
means his head is home
to a spider.

He obsesses
over empty cobwebs,
all those hungry eyes
in the darkness
of his skull.

Declares entomologists assassins.

Says the spider is the soul.

Hard not to think of you
as a tool of divination.

They say your parts can see it all
or near enough to feel like fate.

They've read the bones, the liver, the whole of me
and found the omens unfavourable

the future too difficult to determine
so they break me down again

& again to bring me into being in your image.
Perhaps me breathing is the problem

how your shriek, screech, howl
has me wriggling in your mechanical mouth.

Seeing their frustration, I wonder if your seers
ever envy the old prophets

the way a blade made a body
easy to interpret.

HOLIDAY TRAGEDY

broken ornament
by convulsing body

long-desired heirloom
ruined in a moment

white eyes & shards
reflect the lights

family grief shines
Christmas bright

don't look
here for metaphor

the body is nothing
like the ornament

today beauty moves
small
     the bed as
     balcony
        overlooks
the stage

    a glass
  of water
refracting
  sunshine
into
spotlight
  a dust mote
pirouetting
by the
air
     vent

breathing
breathing
in
applause

BECOMING

there was no becoming
Death had to be born dead
to be itself

I used to dream of thirty-two
that I might live
to be so ancient

what does it mean now
to set aside becoming and be
this man I barely imagined

I hope to turn sixty-two
and not be afraid
to dance naked in the rain

I hope to turn ninety-two
and remain surprised
by who I was and am and might become

I hope to always be
nothing like poor Death
that only ever knew
exactly what it was

(DE)GENERATION

Death was at the table
because of course
it always is. We were in that moment
no more or less aware of it
than you. What else is there to say
except that we were
young & old & maybe pained
or that we played & breathed
& were.

Time has written poems
on your skin.

A lifetime spent
studying their lines
until we too
are poemed
would embody
beauty.

It felt like Communion,
their slow dance in the kitchen.
Somewhere a ghost-voiced radio
played and the song was God
promising *forever*, only
watching them I knew it must be true.

THE EGANVILLE HEALER'S COMPOUND

We went there as a family once. Being secular, I believed
in salvation through the self or science, not charms or
     charlatans.

But when medicine failed me, my mother & father, devout
followers of the church of parenthood, reached out to him

& God & anything they thought could help me. At his
     compound
we found dollars drowning in his wishing well; a counter full of
     prayer

cards & chocolate bars; a wall of postcards proclaiming him a
     god
-ly man; & a platter overburdened with bills, the marks of his
     charity.

In his office, I felt only emptiness at the miracle of his touch.
     And,
he promised, laying on hands was possible even at a distance

through the wonders of technology. Polaroids were the pictures
of faith. They were hung in his chapel like saints & shot

by those who ached with love for the afflicted. Later, my parents
captured me & my pain and mailed us to his compound packed

with their hopes & their money.

UPKEEP

Where it only used to whisper
like wind through a bone
now the old chair creaks
a shrill note under me.

I sit & watch my father
impersonating furniture
with my young niece.
So certain he'd been grandfathered

in to his mother's early end
he'd told me while lying
on the hospital bed
how the time had come
for change.

Now listen to him with my niece.
Together they hit that antique pitch
of finite things that with some upkeep
seem like they might last forever.

PATIENT

waiting

the heart
spites
the call
to still

not / now
not / now
not / now
not / now
not / now

not / now
not / now

not / now

not / now

not

not

not

     now

You gave us pebbles from the seashore, driftwood pale &
    brown.

We peeled the flesh from our fingers, broke the bones off
at the knuckles, set your stones in one by one,
wore driftwood gloves to hold them together.

We carry the weight of salt in our hands. Our fingers ache
    for warm shores.

We kissed your forehead goodbye. The skin like a plastic
    water bottle.

You drifted out to sea
on a raft of our bones.

DEGENERATION

When we speak in the abstract
   of generations dissipating

    Soon, that way of thought will die
    with them

we so often hope
for the extinction only of an other.
Like grammar, exceptions are everywhere:
please, not our parent or pépère. Just the fading of the older.

*

When they speak in the abstract
   of generations degenerating

    Back in my day children weren't,
    well, whatever this is

they so seldom see anything
but themselves. In the absence
of their mother or mémère, the words
of old become their own.

*

When we speak in the abstract
   of generational dealings

         I would or we won't,
         we were or we didn't

we all forget past and future
are not just times or tenses
but languages we think we speak
fluently.

There is a shadow   world in the pendulum
swing of her arms   when her weathered fingers
release the sand bags

Pocket: 200
the hole is a universe deep
and   she is falling fracturing
her bones   like a glass maze   cracking down to
dust   always on the floor

Pocket: 100
the hole is dark   midnight
and a bald stranger in her bed
wipes her tears   says if she waters
her hazelnuts   trees will grow
out of her head

Pocket: 0
she misses the board
her fingers recall
his chest with hair thick like moss the length
of him   she cups the sand bag   just so
smiles knowingly   not remembering
why exactly

Pocket: 500
the hole is light   shining
off the scissors with which   she says
she cut your hair   as you slept
to make you   pay for the curls
she never had

Pocket: 500
the hole is six feet deep
her sister asked   to be buried whole
and not burned to keep   the curls   she mocked her
for and   her husband held her hand   so cold
and he is cold   on the bed
they should loosen   his collar
to let him breathe   to let him breathe
please   let him breathe

Pocket: 500
the hole is an open   mouth
and her tongue throws   words
like sand bags

You are here, still, scattered
among us:
>   your eyes & dinner plates
>   crooked fingers & quilted blankets
>   webbed toes & old oak bookshelves.

Your croaking voice we find in
car crash doors, crows,
and creaking floorboards.

A sound you birthed accidentally as a child
when you drank down burning candle wax

and brought your own voice
screaming into the world.

you say we'll do it right this time. or the next. we have my
lifetime for goodbyes. you won't say dreams are monologues.
your pacemaker too denies death. in a field it beats a steady
here I'm here I'm here I'm here. dreams are the pacemakers
of grief. memory struggles or slows or stops & dreams shock
me to remembrance.

RELIC

There was no escaping your molecules
for a time.

Then, another death. A deeper grief:
        your bedroom's mildew scent
        abandoned the blanket
        we inherited.

So little of you left is left.

But, of course, the afterlife
is in our hair.

On my nightstand is a reliquary:
a novel bookmarked
with a hair strand
from your kitchen floor.

What is a poem
if not hair
spread across a page,
an invitation to believe?

Who even knows
to whom the strand belonged.

Or if it matters in the end.

listen there are peas in my shoes
crushed flat flavoured by my feet
there is a reason the reason is
the angels here are keeping me
keeping us from preparing
for the move to a new home
they say this is my home they call it that
a home they need it to be that and it is
it was but now they want me in a new home
so they cannot retire no but nurse me
me with all my children grandchildren too
how they think i need that is beyond me
and why could you please explain why
there are peas in my shoes yes there are
lists always lists in life and i need to be listed
first for my new home but when i hold
the button for first in the elevator the voice
tells me to let go i need to let go
and the angels come and you must be
an angel here to take away my peas

Youth is not a shield
            but a spell
the illusion that
     for a time
one should be
       immortal
             untouched.

You are too young
     to be so ill.

Why tell me I am wrong
             impossible
as I am
when I am

here.

THE OLD MAN IN HIS ROOM,
ALWAYS IN THE NUDE

The stories they tell in the kitchen
arming themselves
with dinner trays:

> *He clothes himself*
> *only in clouds*
> *of cigarette smoke.*

He is a virgin
desperate
for a fuck.

> *He set fire to his uniform*
> *after the armistice*
> *& forever swore off cotton.*

He is a disgraced
royal of an unknown
dynasty.

> *He exists*
> *only by the grace*
> *of government subsidy.*

He never outgrew
his northern Ontario
cult.

He is the living
embodiment
of toxic male entitlement.

He was in a movie
once, you know,
that one.

He had only a shirt
to gamble with
on Wednesday night poker.

He has dementia eating away
at his sympathy for the staff
but not his appetite.

Maybe he is
exactly who
he says he is.

HOSPITAL TIME

1.
Is this a day
people want or need
their hands
   on you?

2.
"I am the measure of all things."

Seven steps: a space with freedom
to piss in a bowl.

Eleven steps: a glass to oversee a maple
contemplate the parking's symmetry
the disorder leaves might cause come fall.

(They should bring in dirt & trees.
Rooms & bodies need
   the messy stuff
for life.)

Twenty five steps: the insight counter
where you gift the nurses
your wisdom.

3.
Imagine
all roads leading somewhere
    not a bed.

4.
If you are to channel
        pain
you want television's
technicolor range
        in language.
To colour in
    each ache.

5.
That fear of becoming
    just an object
of study.

6.
Time is a dripping
        down
your IV line.

HOSPITAL VISIT

she is half phantom
i am her shadow grandson
friendship makes us blood

TO A DYING FRIEND

You say, *I was so beautiful once*
but I never knew that ancient beauty
only this body like a forest fire
like a field of bones
its boundaries impossible
to distinguish from the bed sheet.

You say, *I wish they'd let me die*
in my red coat
but no, that thin blue robe is home.

You say, *We are not really*
here, in this now
and, true, together we are Janus.

You say, *Tell me stories*
I give you your words
a fashionista on a Vespa teasing dreams
and gas money out of officers
a fabric stitcher with gods in her needle
a friend asking for a final sip
of whisky from my flask.

You say, *Let us now drink*
that great unknown
yes, here's to all those stories never told.

NOTES AND ACKNOWLEDGMENTS

Versions of some of these poems appeared in the following publications: *The Literary Review of Canada, The Puritan,* PRISM *International, Riddle Fence,* EVENT, *The Antigonish Review, This* magazine, *Canadian Medical Association Journal (*CMAJ*), Geez, Bywords, Plenitude, Wordgathering, Uncanny* magazine, *Strange Horizons, The Quilliad, Goblin Fruit, inkscrawl, Glass: A Poetry Journal, Poetry Pause, The anti-languorous review,* GUEST, *Big Smoke Poetry, Train, Yes Poetry, Atticus Review,* and BOAAT. Some of the poems were originally published in *We, Old Young Ones,* a chapbook printed by Frog Hollow Press. My thanks to all the editors for their support.

"Bilingual pathways": the line "French people are so hardcore they eat pain for breakfast" comes from a popular internet meme. The words usually accompany an image of bread as a play on the French word for bread: pain.

"With apologies to those with congenital analgesia": According to the US National Library of Medicine, "Congenital insensitivity to pain is a condition that inhibits the ability to perceive physical pain. From birth, affected individuals never feel pain in any part of their body when injured … This lack of pain awareness often leads to an accumulation of wounds, bruises, broken bones, and other health issues that may go undetected."

"My partner makes of me a poem": this poem was created by taking snippets of strange and wonderful things my then partner Kelsi Morris said about my body over the course of our relationship.

"You came to say goodbye again": the idea of a pacemaker continuing to function after death came from Dr Eric Van De Graaff's article "Pacemakers and Death."

"The Eganville healer's compound": Richard Dale, a self-professed faith healer, ran the Dal-Grotto Mission in Eganville, ON, for over fifty years.

"Hospital time": the line "I am the measure of all things" was borrowed from Leena Krohn's novel *Tainaron: Mail from Another City*.

I owe a great debt to Dr Shane Neilson and Roxanna Bennett, both excellent humans and poets. Shane's research on pain has been invaluable in helping me approach pain in my own work, and his writing and support of the disabled community have had a great impact on my life and my career. Roxanna's writing and correspondence have been a joy and a balm for my days, and her friendship has helped my work reach new heights. No single work of poetry has ever resonated with me quite as deeply as her chapbook *unseen garden* and later her collection *unmeaningable*. Anyone interested in disability poetics in Canada and in general would do well to find the work of these remarkably talented people.

I am very grateful to Allan Hepburn, Carolyn Smart, Mark Abley, Kathleen Fraser, and the entire McGill-Queen's University Press team. Thank you also to David Drummond for the beautiful cover.

My heartfelt thanks to Terese Mason Pierre, Elsa Sjunneson, Shazia Hafiz Ramji, John Williamson, K.S.Y. Varnam, Ally Fleming, Kirby and knife | fork | book, Erin Soros, and Andrew Sullivan. All my love and thanks to Jen Albert for all she does.

A thousand thank yous to Dr Stephanie Kwok – you are a credit to your profession. Thanks as well to the medical team at Women's College Hospital and the wonderful people at Nova Pharmacy.

I'm so grateful to the Ontario Arts Council and the various recommender publishers for their support as I worked on this manuscript and others. It's changed my life.

To my family: you continue to make it all possible. You have my love and gratitude, now and always.

Finally, to all my disabled friends and colleagues: your work matters, your lives matter.